HAL•LEONARD

BASS

PLAY•ALONG™

VOL. 38

T0077129

AVENGED SEVENFOLD

Cover photo courtesy of Warner Bros. Records

ISBN 978-1-4584-0494-7

HAL•LEONARD®
CORPORATION
7777 W. BLUEMOUND RD. P.O. BOX 13819 MILWAUKEE, WI 53213

In Australia Contact:
Hal Leonard Australia Pty. Ltd.
4 Lentara Court
Cheltenham, Victoria, 3192 Australia
Email: ausadmin@halleonard.com.au

Visit Hal Leonard Online at
www.halleonard.com

CONTENTS

Page	Title	Demo Track	Play-Along Track
6	Afterlife	1	2
18	Almost Easy	3	4
38	Bat Country	5	6
52	Beast and the Harlot	7	8
27	Nightmare	9	10
64	Scream	11	12
72	Unholy Confessions	13	14
	TUNING NOTES	15	

BASS NOTATION LEGEND

Bass music can be notated two different ways: on a *musical staff*, and in *tablature*

Notes:

THE MUSICAL STAFF shows pitches and rhythms and is divided by bar lines into measures. Pitches are named after the first seven letters of the alphabet.

TABLATURE graphically represents the bass fingerboard. Each horizontal line represents a string, and each number represents a fret.

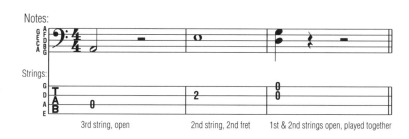

3rd string, open   2nd string, 2nd fret   1st & 2nd strings open, played together

---

HAMMER-ON: Strike the first (lower) note with one finger, then sound the higher note (on the same string) with another finger by fretting it without picking.

PULL-OFF: Place both fingers on the notes to be sounded. Strike the first note and without picking, pull the finger off to sound the second (lower) note.

LEGATO SLIDE: Strike the first note and then slide the same fret-hand finger up or down to the second note. The second note is not struck.

SHIFT SLIDE: Same as legato slide, except the second note is struck.

TRILL: Very rapidly alternate between the notes indicated by continuously hammering on and pulling off.

TREMOLO PICKING: The note is picked as rapidly and continuously as possible.

VIBRATO: The string is vibrated by rapidly bending and releasing the note with the fretting hand.

SHAKE: Using one finger, rapidly alternate between two notes on one string by sliding either a half-step above or below.

NATURAL HARMONIC: Strike the note while the fret hand lightly touches the string directly over the fret indicated.

MUFFLED STRINGS: A percussive sound is produced by laying the fret hand across the string(s) without depressing them and striking them with the pick hand.

BEND: Strike the note and bend up the interval shown.

BEND AND RELEASE: Strike the note and bend up as indicated, then release back to the original note. Only the first note is struck.

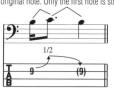

RIGHT-HAND TAP: Hammer ("tap") the fret indicated with the "pick-hand" index or middle finger and pull off to the note fretted by the fret hand.

LEFT-HAND TAP: Hammer ("tap") the fret indicated with the "fret-hand" index or middle finger.

SLAP: Strike ("slap") string with right-hand thumb.

POP: Snap ("pop") string with right-hand index or middle finger.

Additional Musical Definitions

(accent) • Accentuate note (play it louder)

(accent) • Accentuate note with great intensity

(staccato) • Play the note short

D.S. al Coda • Go back to the sign (𝄋), then play until the measure marked **"To Coda"**, then skip to the section labelled **"Coda."**

Fill • Label used to identify a brief pattern which is to be inserted into the arrangement.

• Repeat measures between signs.

• When a repeated section has different endings, play the first ending only the first time and the second ending only the second time.

Afterlife

Words and Music by Matthew Sanders, James Sullivan, Brian Haner, Jr. and Zachary Baker

Drop D tuning:
(low to high) D-A-D-G

Intro

Moderately ♩ = 110

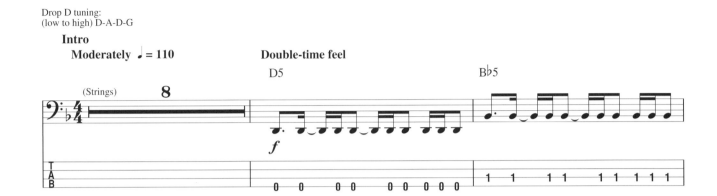

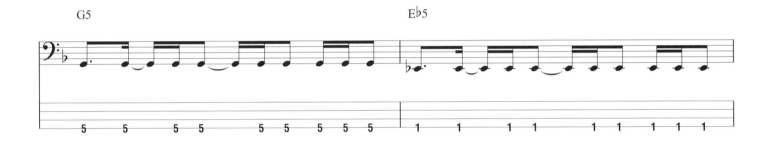

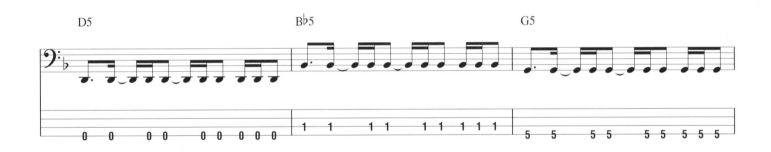

End double-time feel

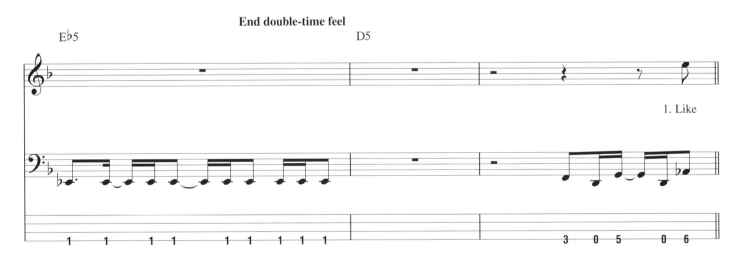

% Verse

walk - ing in - to a dream, _____ so un - like _ what you've seen. _____

2. *See additional lyrics*

So un - sure ___ but it seems, _____ 'cause we've been wait - ing for you.

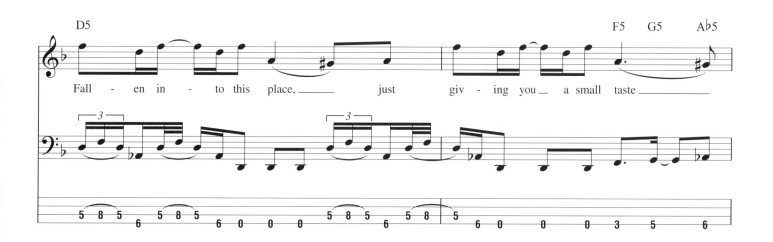

Fall - en in - to this place, _____ just giv - ing you _ a small taste _____

of your af - ter-life here, so stay. _____ You'll be back _ here soon an - y - way. _____

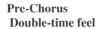

Pre-Chorus
Double-time feel

I see a dis - tant __ light, __
See additional lyrics

but, girl, this can't be __ right. __

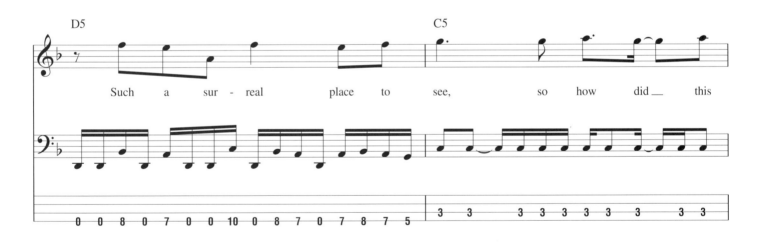

Such a sur - real place to see, so how did __ this

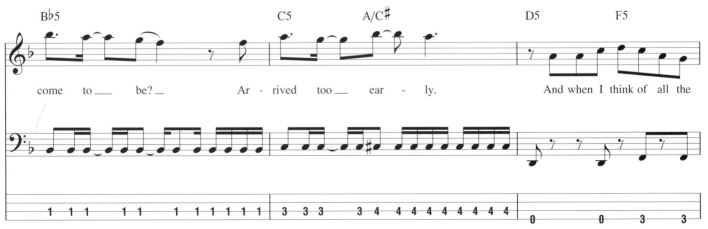

come to __ be? __ Ar - rived too __ ear - ly. And when I think of all the

⊕ Coda
Chorus
Half-time feel

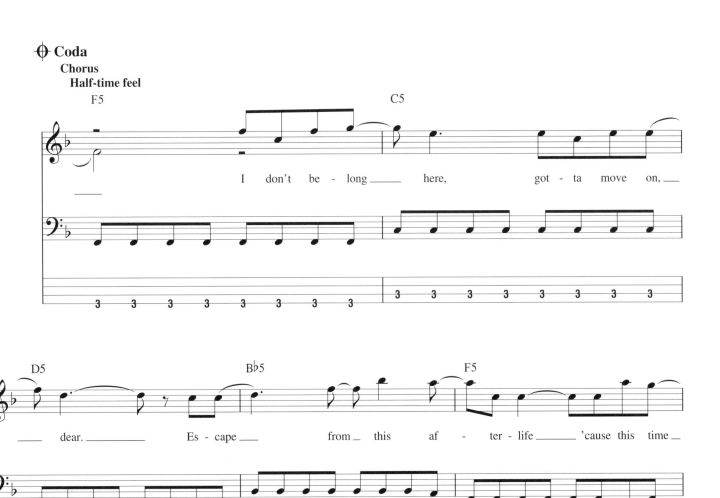

I don't be-long _____ here, got-ta move on, _____ dear. _____ Es-cape _____ from ___ this af - ter-life _____ 'cause this time __

End half-time feel

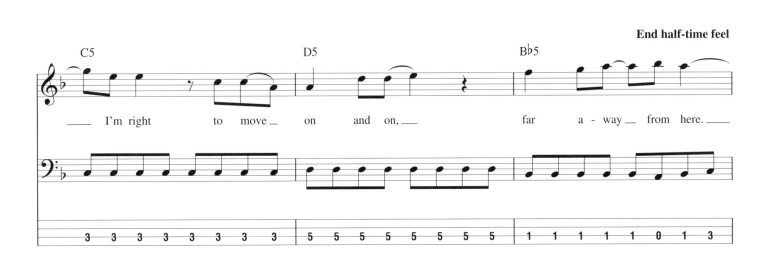

_____ I'm right to move __ on and on, ___ far a - way __ from here. ___

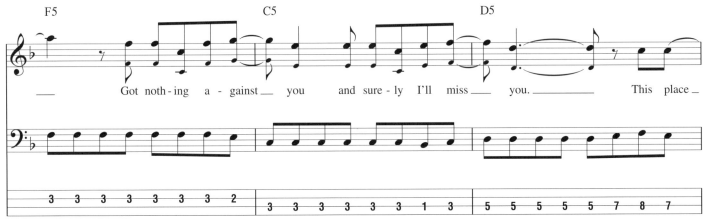

_____ Got noth-ing a - gainst ___ you and sure-ly I'll miss ___ you. _____ This place ___

full __ of peace __ and light, _____ and I thought __ you might take me

back in - side __ when the time __ is right. _____

Interlude
Half-time feel

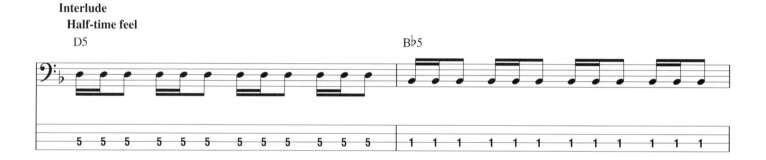

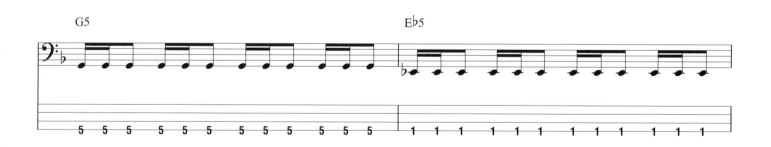

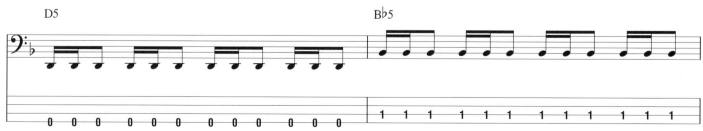

per - son I wan - na be. ____ Oh, Lord, I'll

I'm chok - ing on the ec - sta - sy. ____ Un - break me,

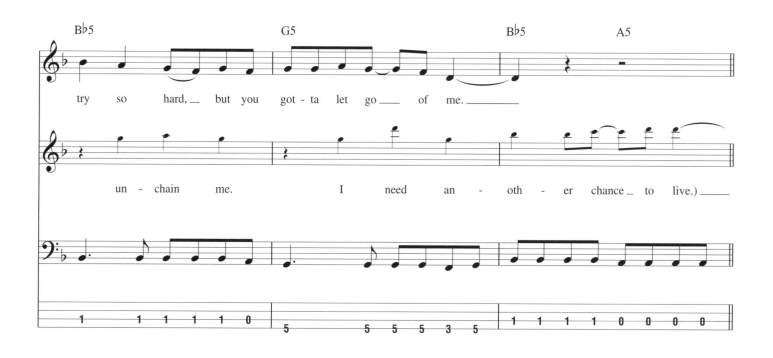

try so hard, __ but you got - ta let go ___ of me. _____

un - chain me. I need an - oth - er chance __ to live.) ____

Guitar Solo
Double-time feel

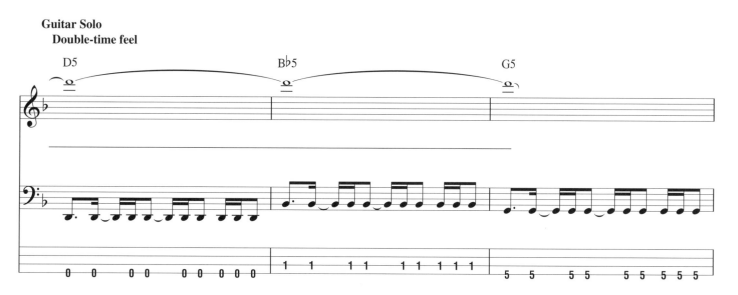

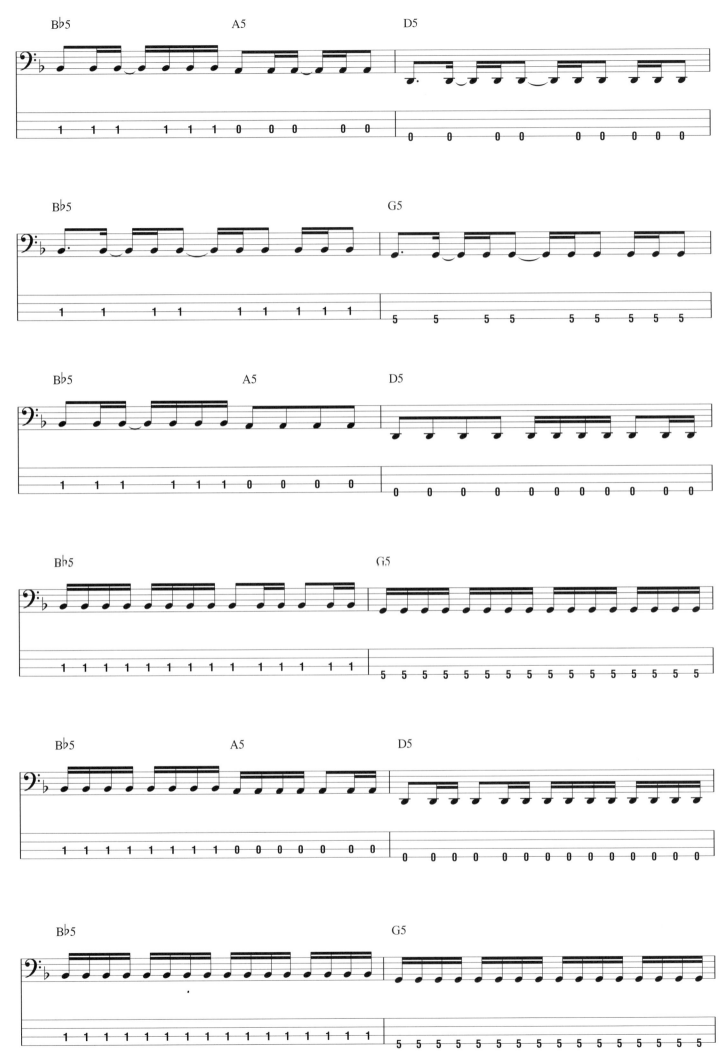

14

Interlude
End double-time feel

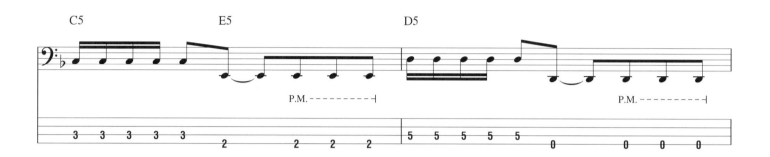

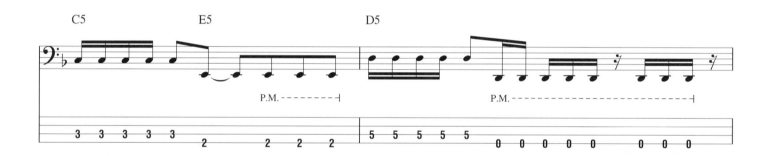

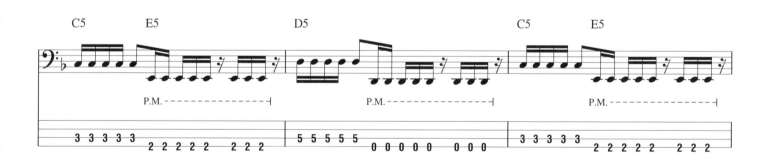

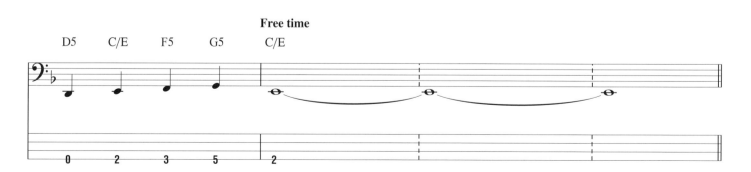

Chorus

I don't be - long ___ here, got - ta move on, ___ dear. ___ Es - cape ___

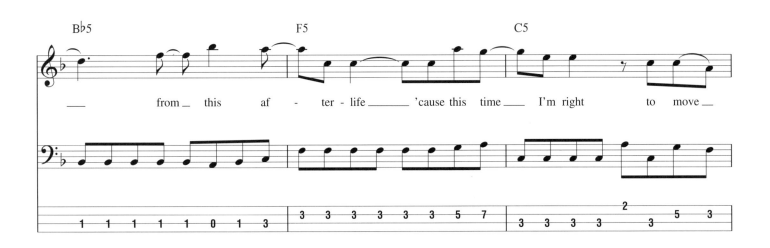

___ from ___ this af - ter - life ___ 'cause this time ___ I'm right to move ___

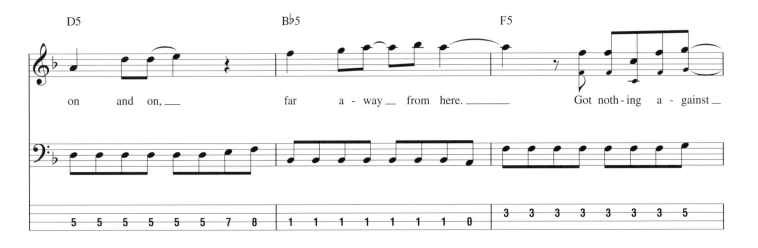

on and on, ___ far a - way ___ from here. ___ Got noth - ing a - gainst ___

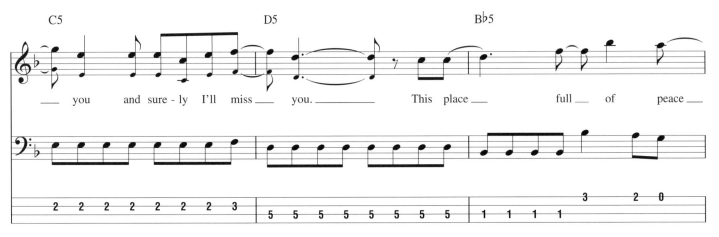

___ you and sure - ly I'll miss ___ you. ___ This place ___ full ___ of peace ___

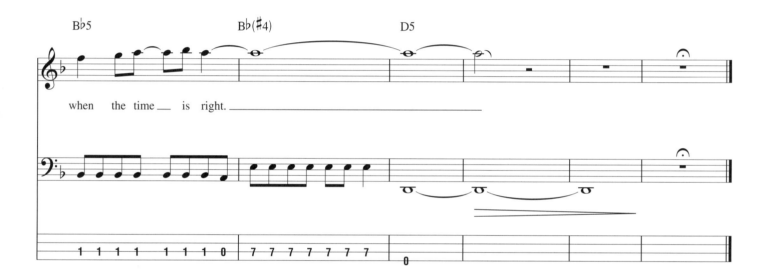

Additional Lyrics

2. Place of hope and no pain,
   Perfect skies with no rain.
   Can leave this place but refrain,
   'Cause we've been waiting for you.
   Fallen into this place,
   Just giving you a small taste
   Of your afterlife here, so stay.
   You'll be back here soon anyway.

Pre-Chorus   This peace on earth's not right. (With my back against the wall.)
   No pain or sign of time. (I'm much too young to fall.)
   So out of place, don't wanna stay.
   I feel wrong and that's my sign.
   I've made up my mind.
   Give my your hand, but realize I just wanna say goodbye.
   Please understand I have to leave and carry on my own life.

Almost Easy

Words and Music by Matthew Sanders, James Sullivan, Brian Haner, Jr. and Zachary Baker

Drop D tuning, down 1/2 step:
(low to high) D♭-A♭-D♭-G♭

Intro
Moderately fast ♩ = 176

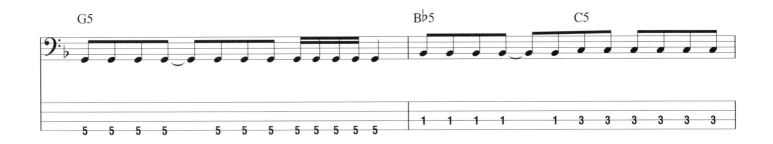

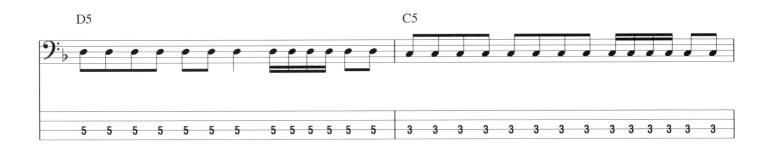

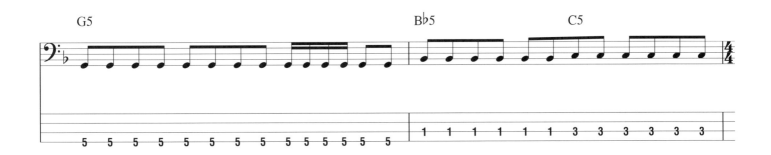

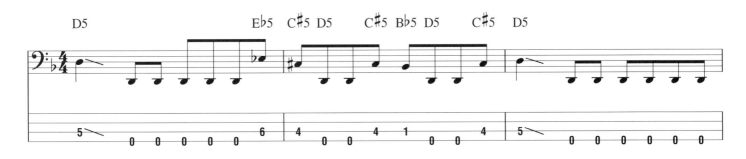

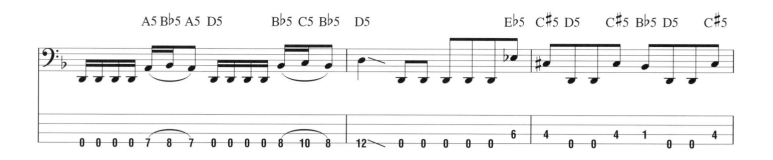

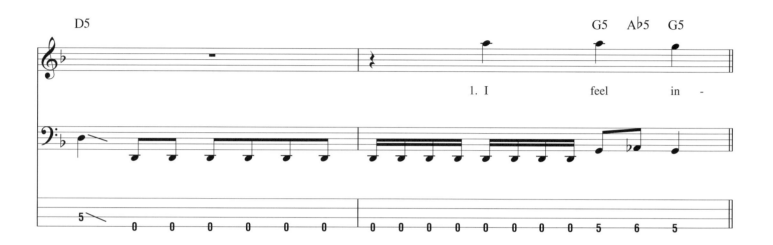

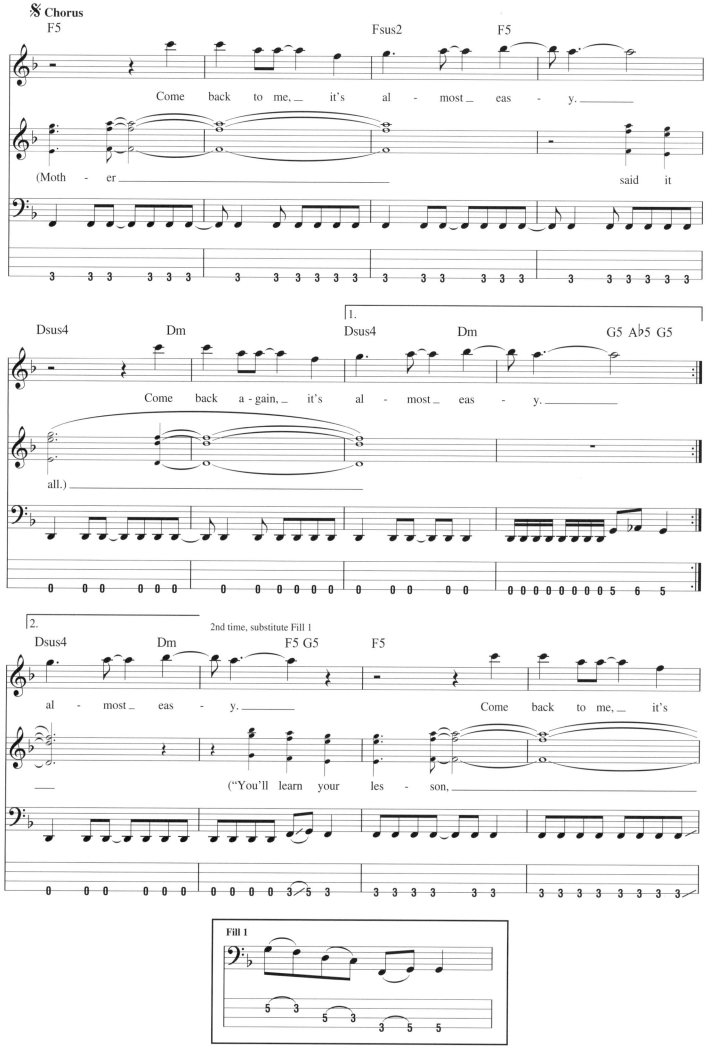

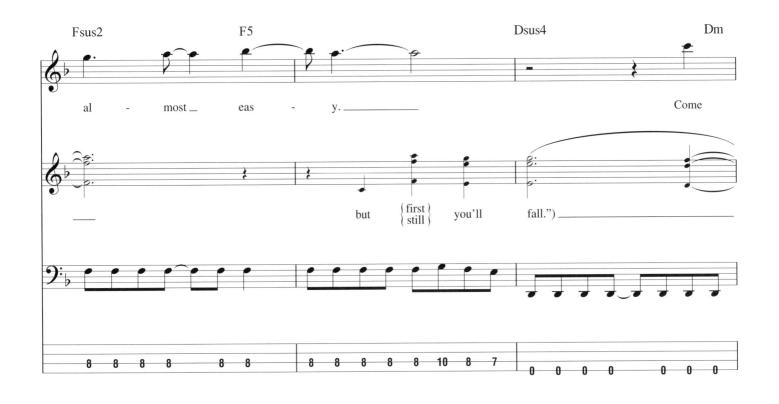

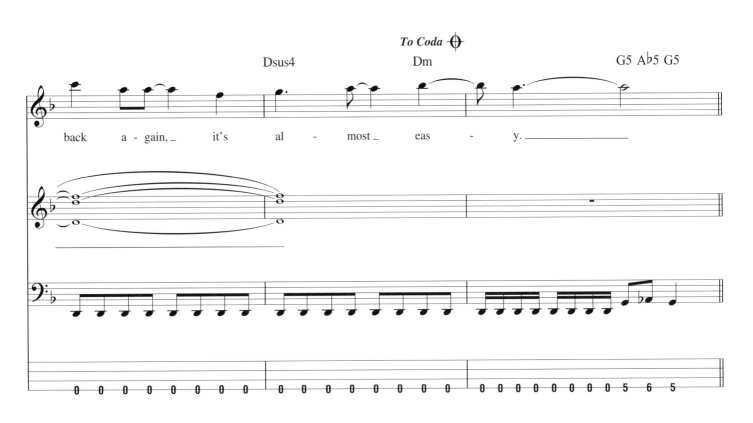

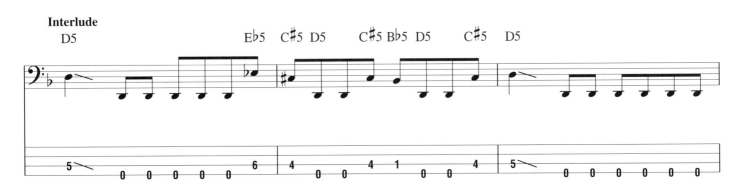

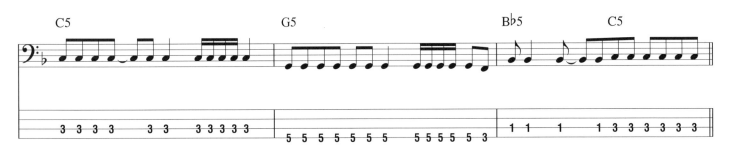

C5   G5   Bb5   C5

Bridge
Half-time feel

D5   F5

Now   that I've   lost you,   it   kills me   to say,   I
                                                                               (Hurts to

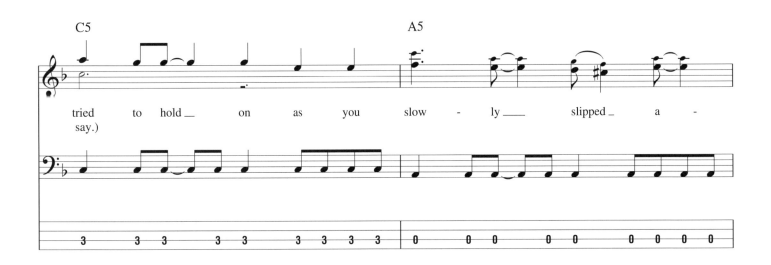

C5   A5

tried   to   hold on   as you   slow - ly   slipped a -
say.)

Bb5   F5

way.   I'm los - in' the fight,   I've
                                           (Ah.

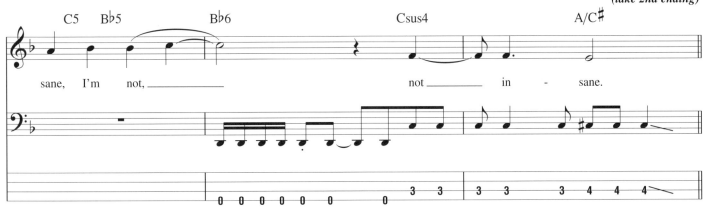

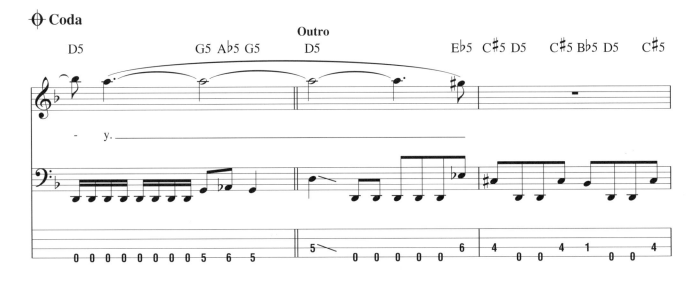

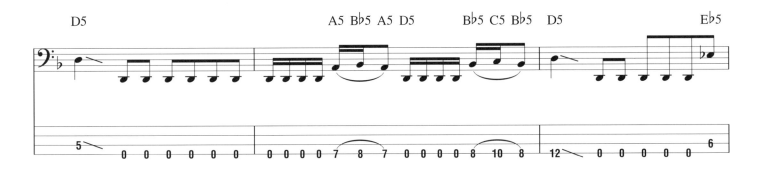

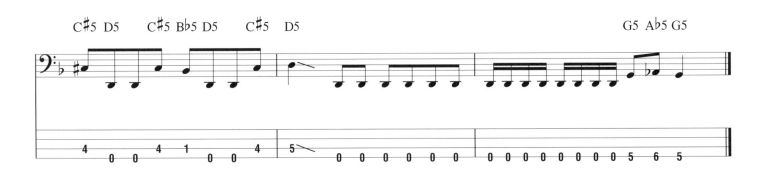

Additional Lyrics

2. Shame pulses through my heart from the things I've done to you.
It's hard to face, but the fact remains that this is nothing new.
I left you bound and tied with suicidal memories.
Selfish beneath the skin, but deep inside I'm not insane.

Nightmare

Words and Music by Matthew Sanders, Jonathan Seward, James Sullivan, Brian Haner, Jr. and Zachary Baker

Now _ your night - mare comes _ to life. _____

Verse

1. Dragged you down be - low,   down to the Dev - il's show _
2. *See additional lyrics*

to be his guest for - ev - er. _____ Peace of mind is less than nev - er! _____

Hate to twist your mind,   but God ain't on your side. _

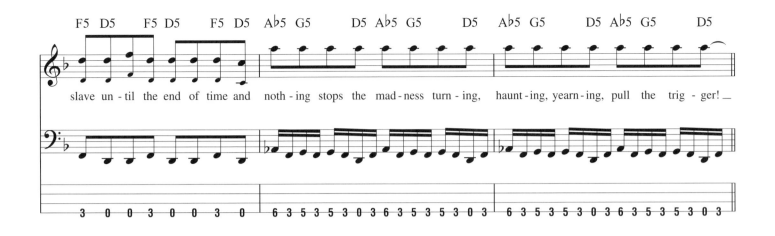

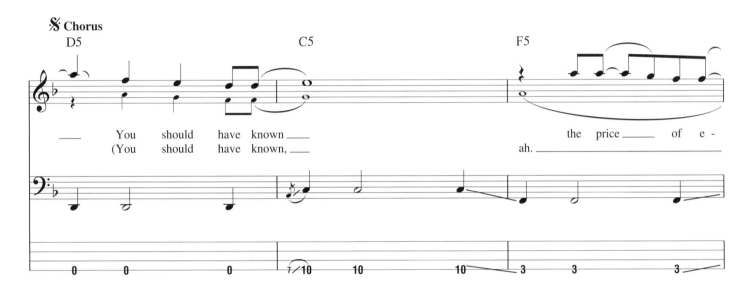

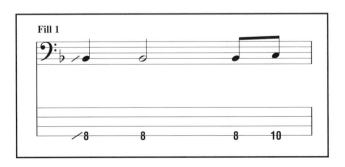

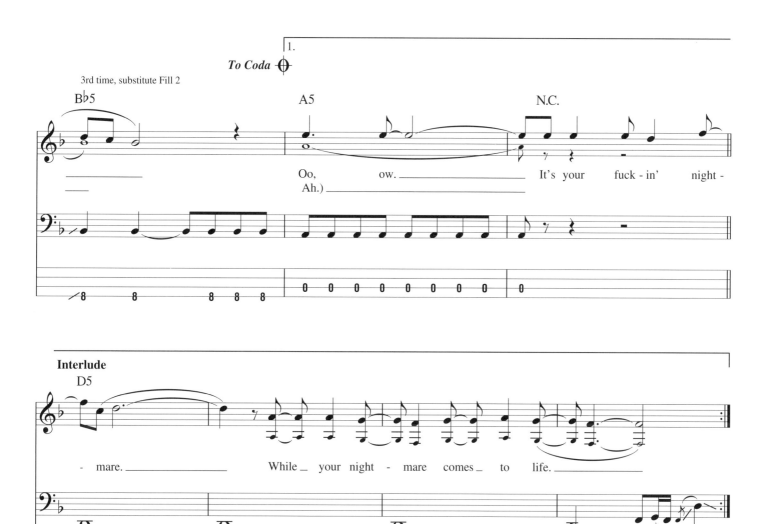

Interlude

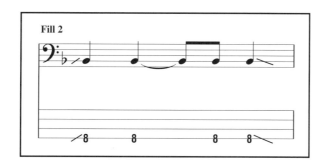

Your trag-ic fate ___ is look-in' so ___ clear, ___ yeah. ___
Your trag-ic fate ___ is look-in' so ___ clear. ___

Oo, ___ ow. ___ It's your fuck-in' night - mare, ___ ha, ha, ha, ha.
Ah.) ___

Interlude

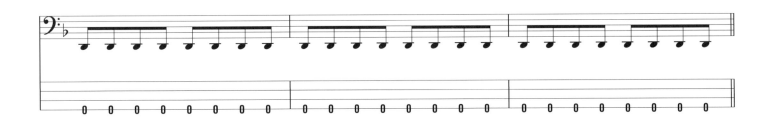

Bridge

Down,   feel   the   fire,   feel   the   hate.   Your pain is   what we de-sire. __

(Down.   Fire.   Hate.

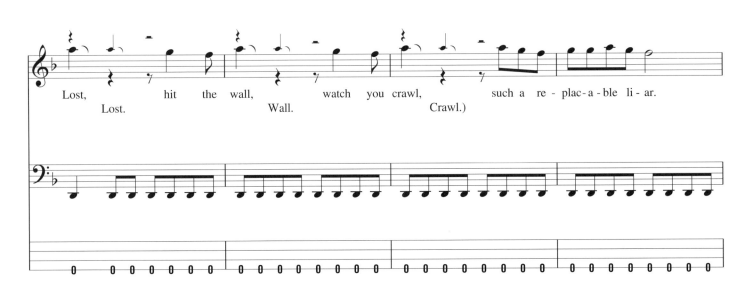

Lost,   hit   the   wall,   watch you crawl,   such a re - plac-a-ble li - ar.

Lost.   Wall.   Crawl.)

Half-time feel

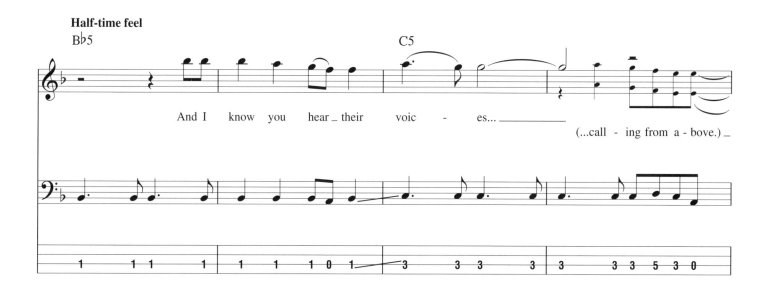

And I know you hear _ their voic - es... _____

(...call - ing from a - bove.) _

And I know they may _ seem real,... _____

_____

(...these sig - nals of love.) _

But our life's made up _ of choic - es,... _____

_____

(...some with - out ap - peal.) _

They took for grant-ed your soul, _____ and it's ours now _ to steal _

D.S. al Coda

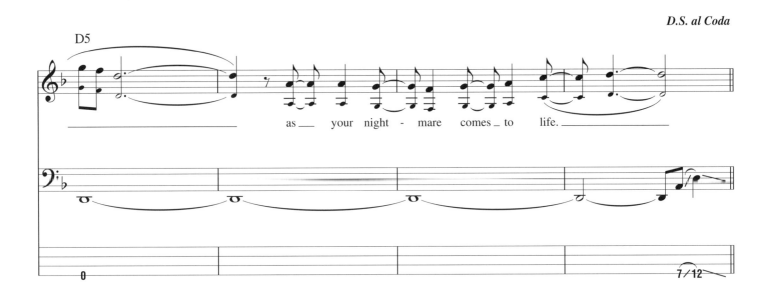

as _ your night - mare comes _ to life. _____

𝄌 **Coda**

Half-time feel

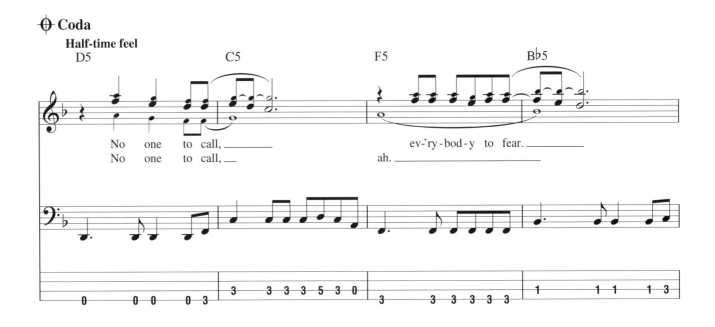

No one to call, _____ ev'-ry-bod-y to fear. _____
No one to call, _ ah. _____

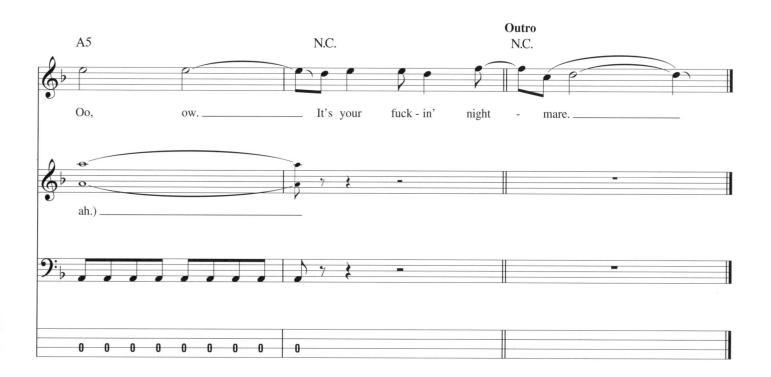

Additional Lyrics

2. Can't wake up in sweat 'cause it ain't over yet.
   Still dancin' with your demons. (Victim of your own creation!)
   Beyond the will to fight, where all that's wrong is right,
   Where hate don't need a reason. (Loathing self-assassination!)
   You've been lied to just to rape you of your sight.
   And now they have the nerve to tell you how to feel. (Feel.)
   So sedated as they medicate your brain, and while you slowly go insane they tell ya,
   "Given with the best intentions, help you with your complications!"

Bat Country

Words and Music by Matthew Sanders, James Sullivan, Brian Haner, Jr. and Zachary Baker

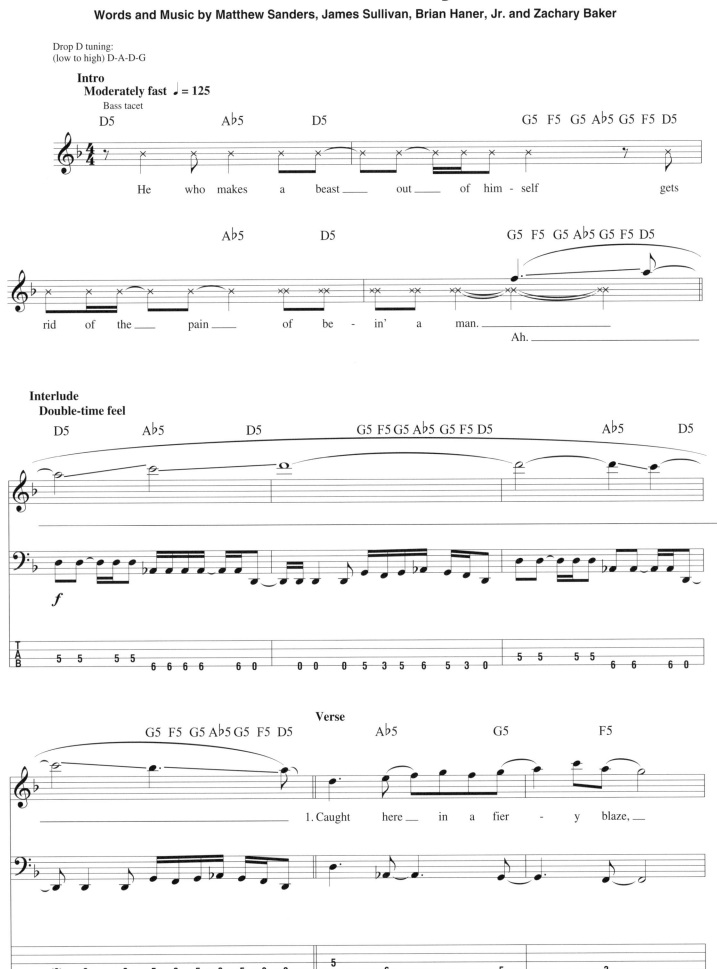

% Pre-Chorus

End double-time feel

death - less words to _____ Can't you help me as I'm start-ing to burn? _

me. _ }

free. _ }

(All _ a -

*Sing upstemmed voc. 1st & 2nd times only.

Too man - y dos - es and I'm start-ing to get an at-trac - tion. _ My con - fi - dence is leav - ing

lone.) _____

To Coda 1

To Coda 2

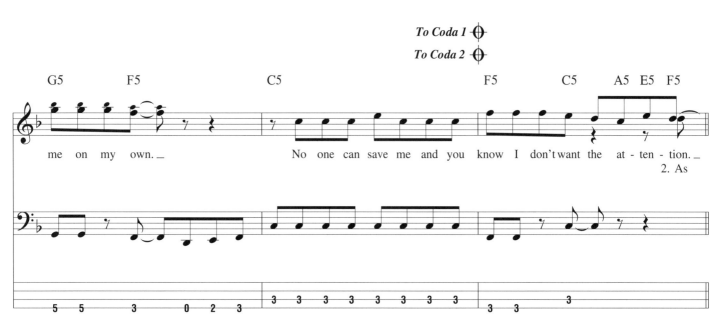

me on my own. _ No one can save me and you know I don't want the at - ten - tion. _

2. As

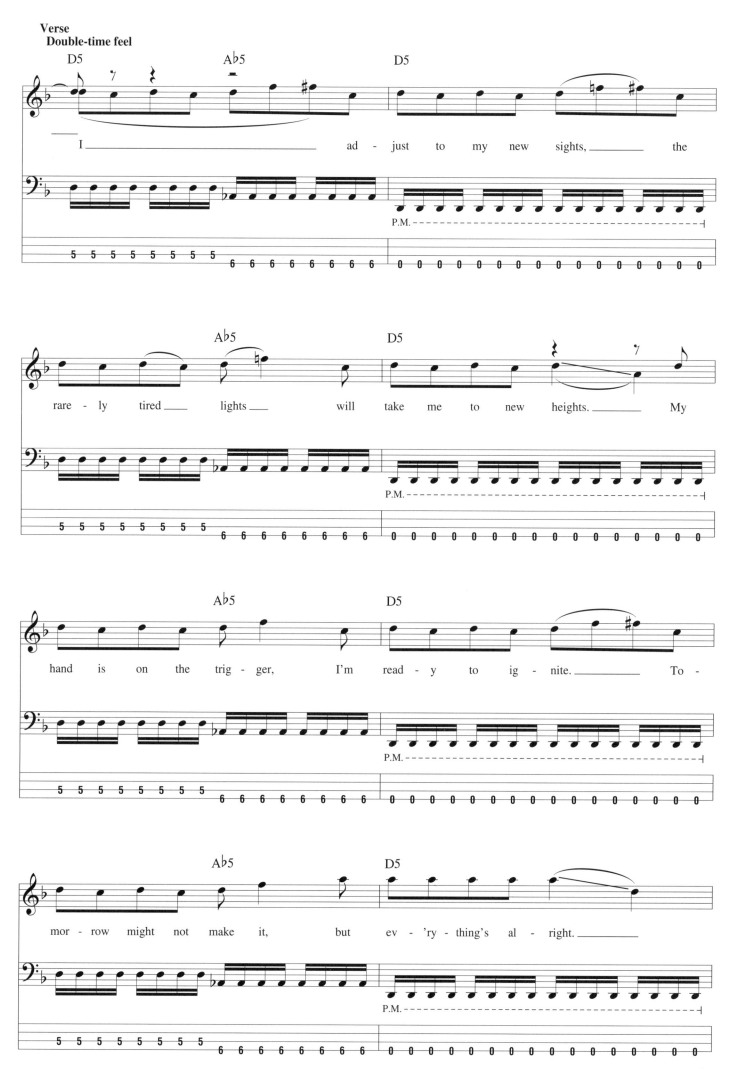

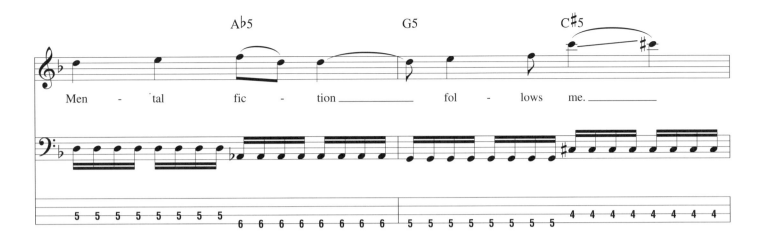

Men - tal fic - tion _____ fol - lows me. _____

D.S. al Coda 1
End double-time feel

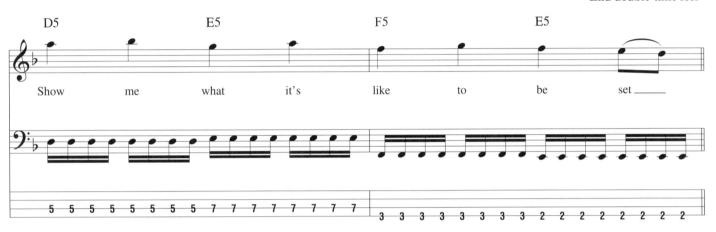

Show me what it's like to be set _____

Coda 1

Chorus
Half-time feel

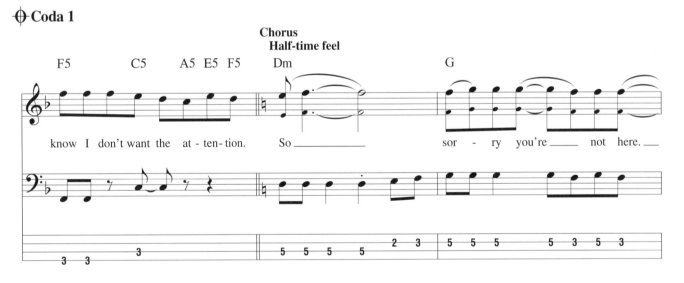

know I don't want the at - ten-tion. So _____ sor - ry you're _____ not here. _____

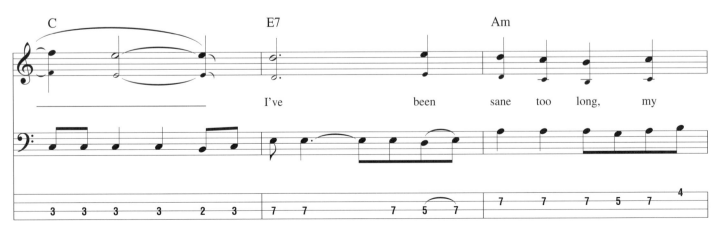

I've been sane too long, my

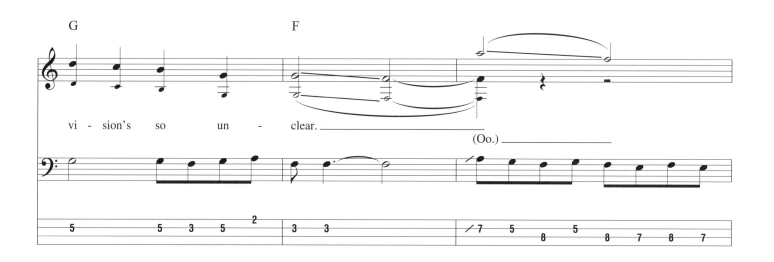

vi - sion's so un - clear. _____

(Oo.) _____

Now, _____ take _ a trip _____ with me, _____

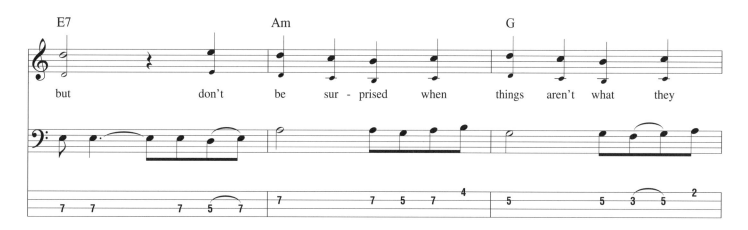

but don't be sur - prised when things aren't what they

Verse
End half-time feel

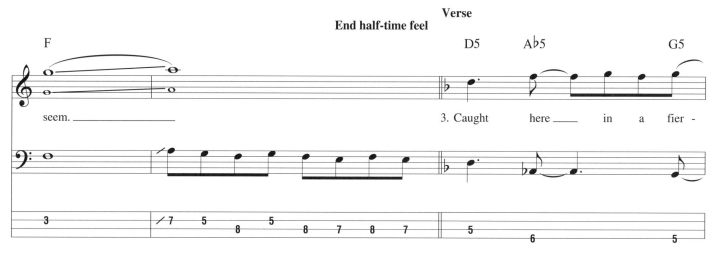

seem. _____ 3. Caught here _____ in a fier -

- y blaze, ___ won't lose ___ my will ___ to stay. ___

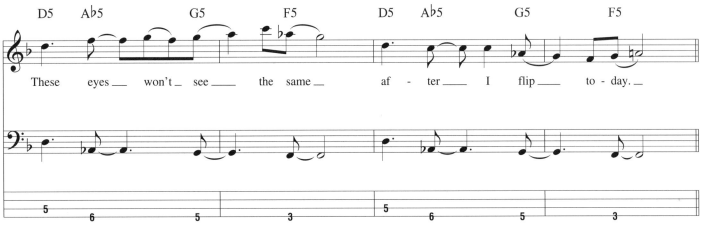

These eyes ___ won't ___ see ___ the same ___ af - ter ___ I flip ___ to - day. ___

Guitar Solo

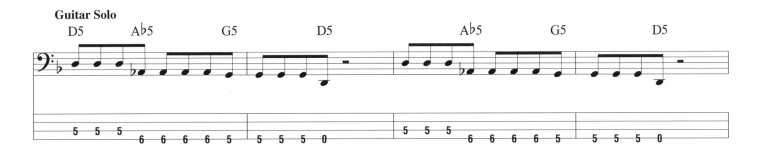

Double-time feel

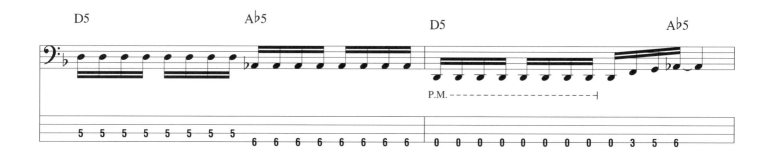

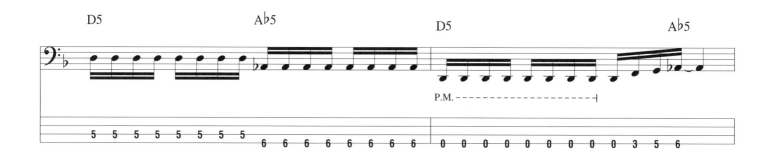

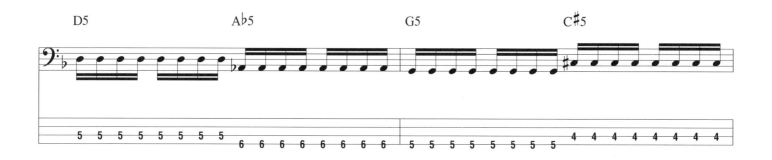

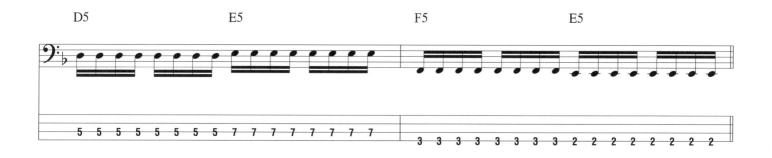

Interlude

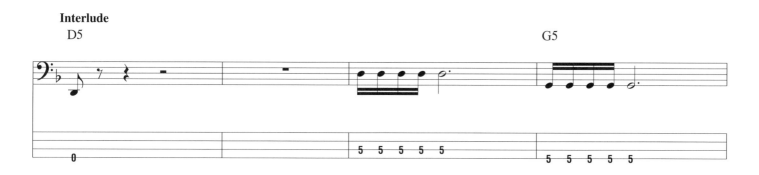

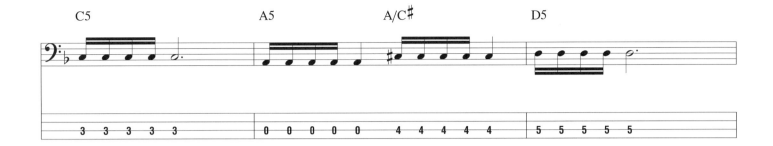

End double-time feel

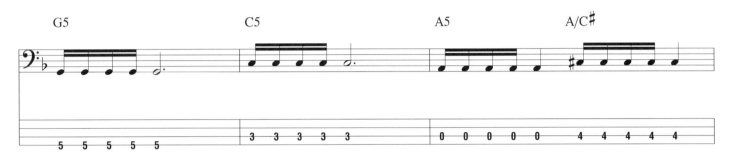

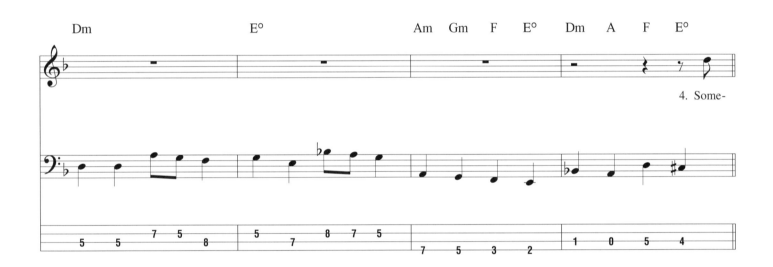

4. Some-

Verse
Double-time feel

times I don't know why _____ we'd rath - er live than die. _____ We

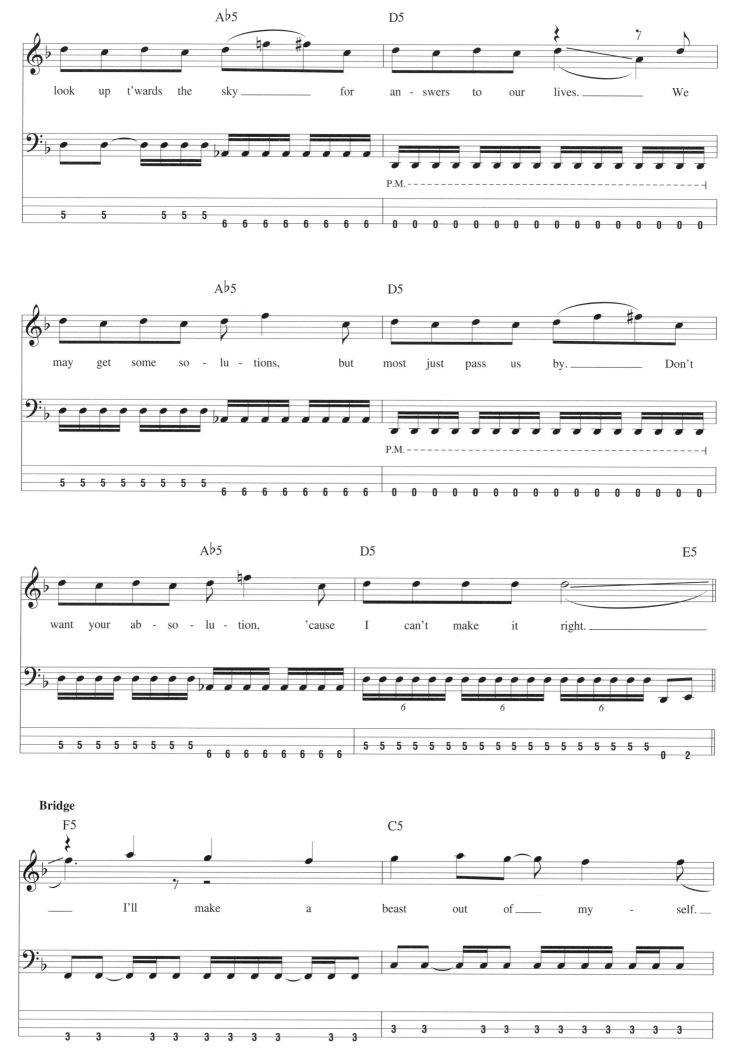

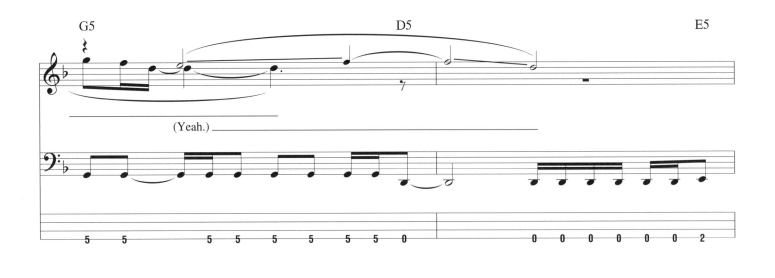

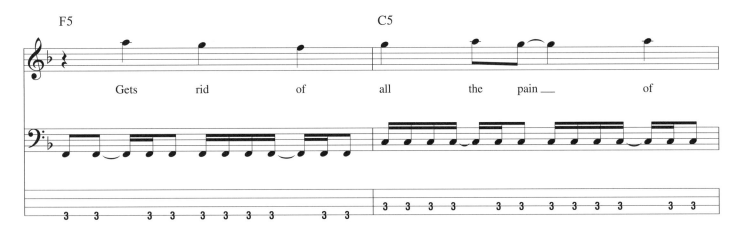

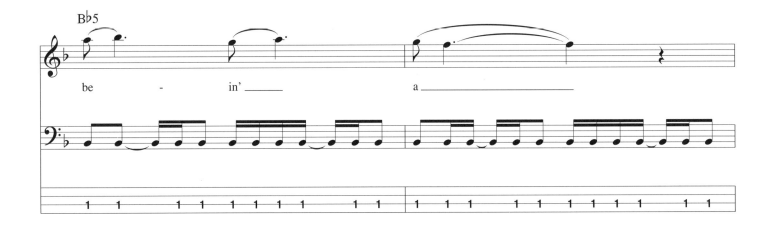

D.S. al Coda 2
End double-time feel

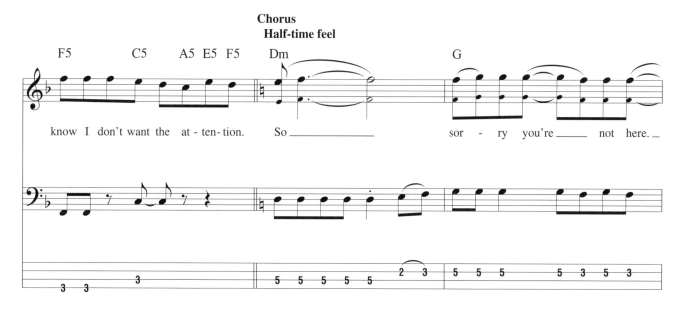

Chorus
Half-time feel

know I don't want the at-ten-tion. So _____ sor - ry you're ____ not here. _

_____ I've been sane too long, my

vi - sion's so un - clear. _____

(Oo.) _____

Now, _____ take _ a trip _____ with me, _____

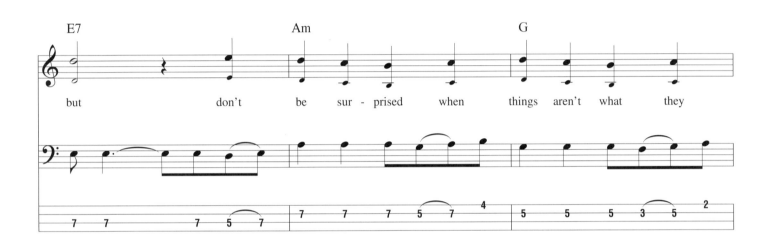

but _____ don't be sur - prised when things aren't what they

End half-time feel

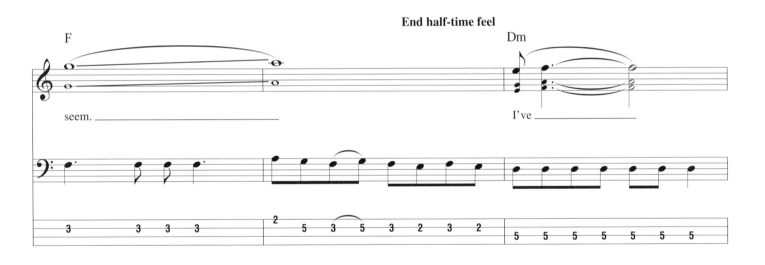

seem. _____ I've _____

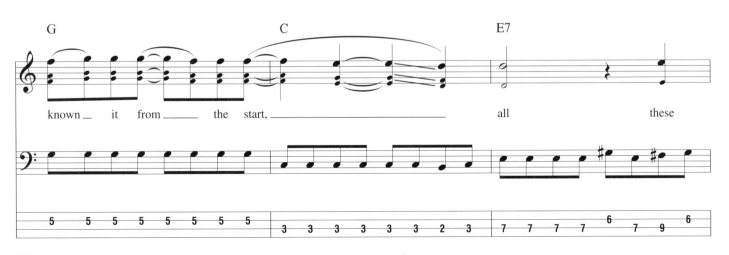

known _ it from _____ the start, _____ all these

Beast and the Harlot

Words and Music by Matthew Sanders, James Sullivan, Brian Haner, Jr. and Zachary Baker

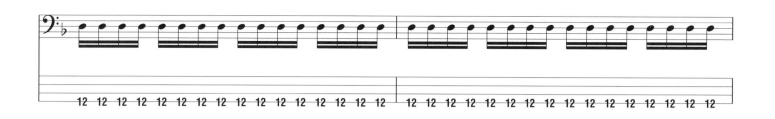

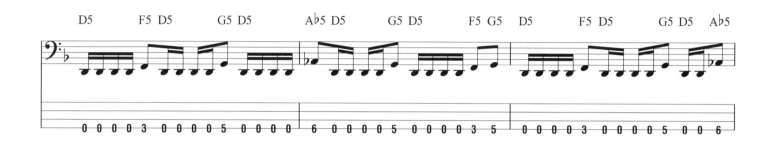

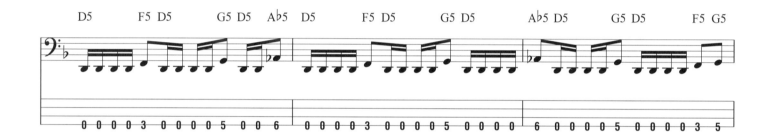

Verse

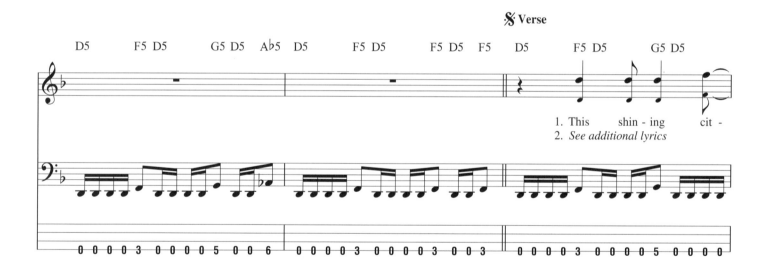

1. This shin-ing cit-
2. *See additional lyrics*

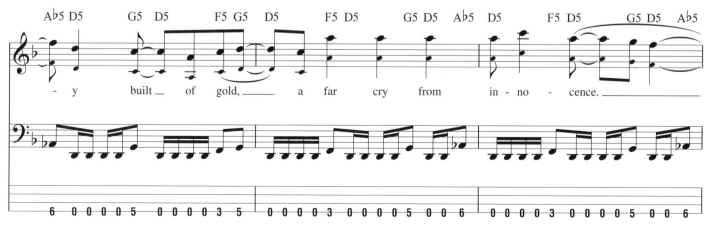

-y built of gold, a far cry from in-no-cence.

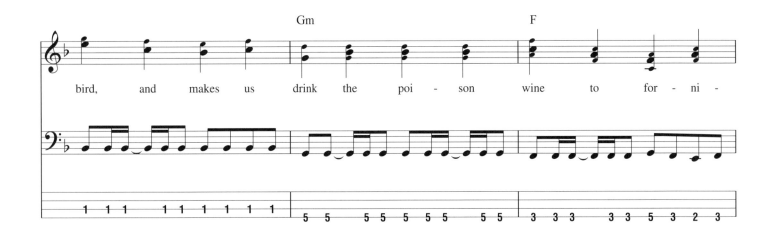

bird, and makes us drink the poi - son wine to for - ni -

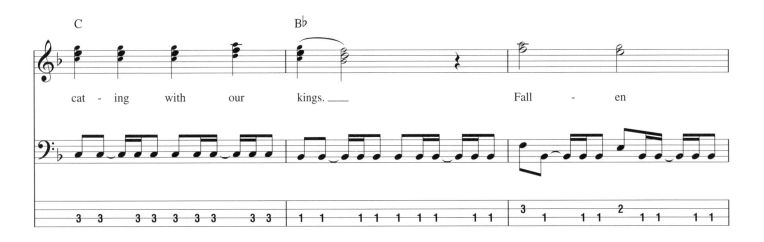

cat - ing with our kings. ___ Fall - en

End double-time feel

To Coda 2 ⊕   *To Coda 1* ⊕

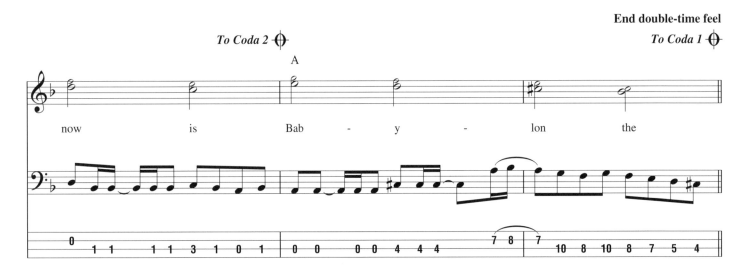

now is Bab - y - lon the

Guitar Solo

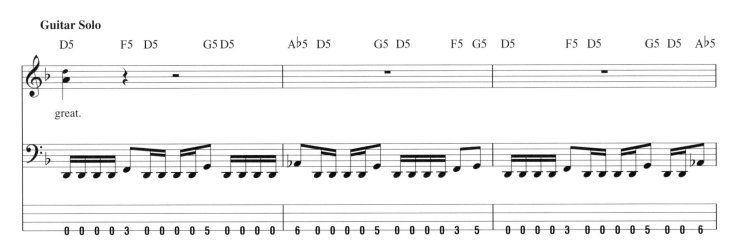

great.

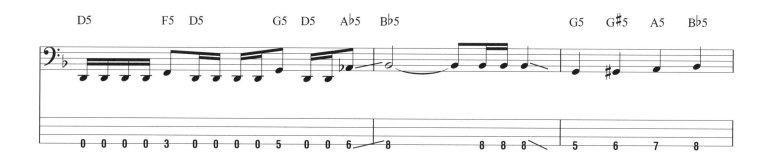

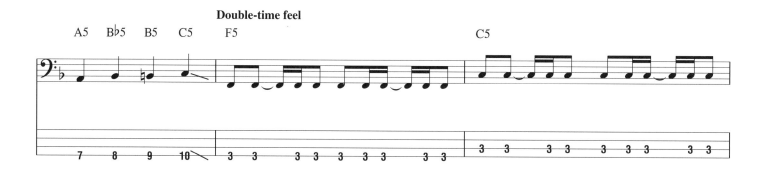

Double-time feel

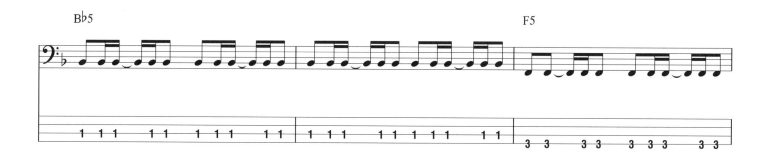

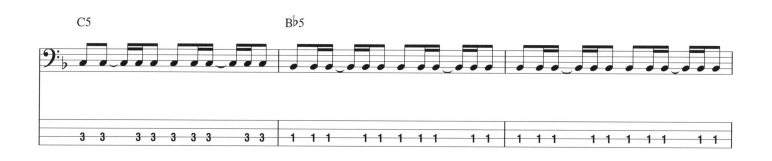

Bb5

D.S. al Coda 1
End double-time feel

A5   A/C#

 Coda 1
Interlude
D5

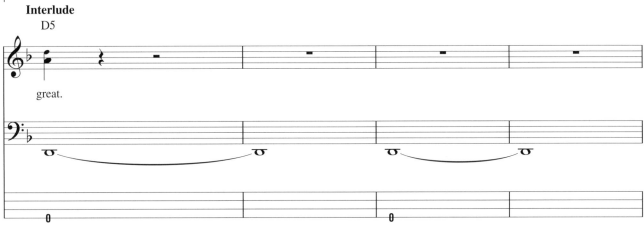

great.

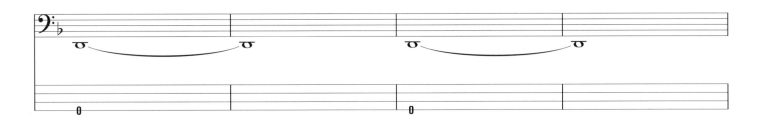

F5 D5   G5 D5   Ab5 D5   G5 D5   F5 G5   D5   F5 D5   G5 D5   Ab5 D5   G5 D5   F5 G5

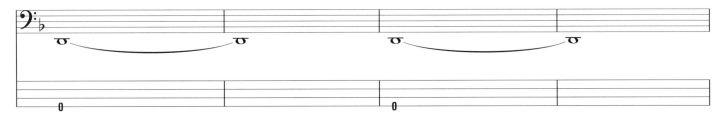

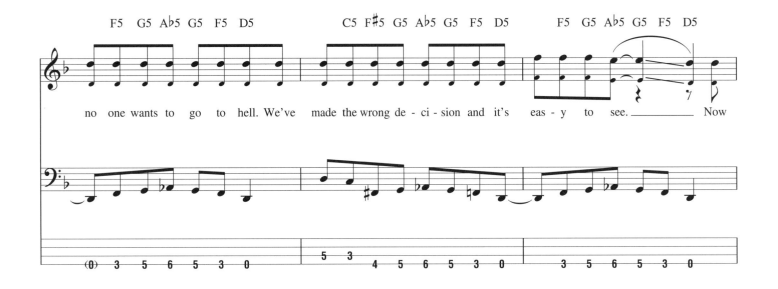

no one wants to go to hell. We've made the wrong de - ci - sion and it's eas - y to see. _____ Now

if you wan - na serve a - bove or be a king be - low with us, you're wel - come to the cit - y where your

fu - ture is set _____ for - ev - - er. _____

(Ah.) _____

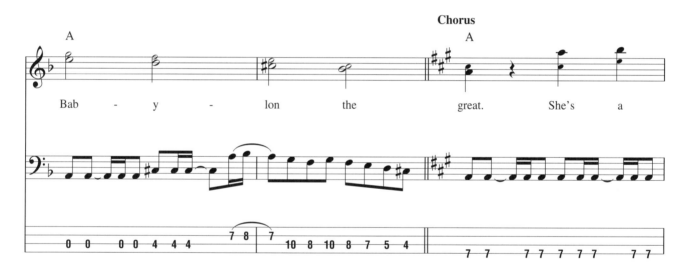

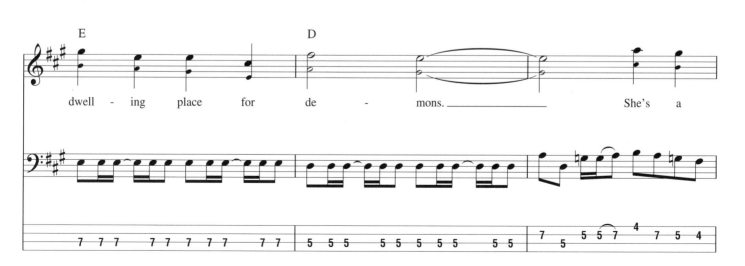

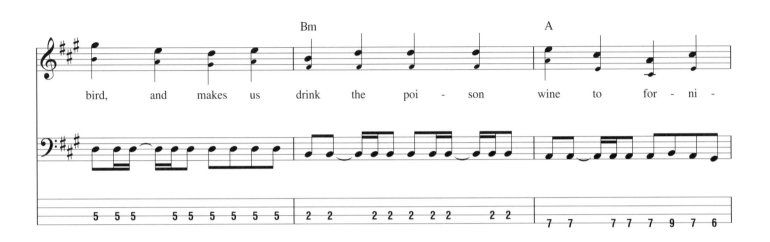

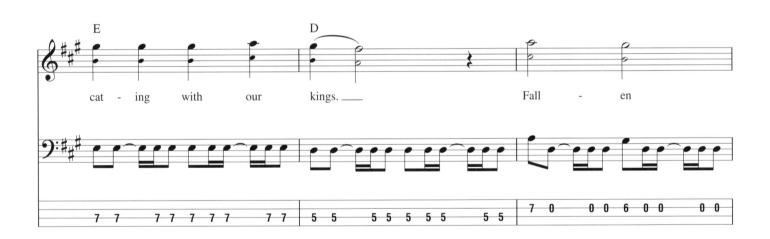

End double-time feel

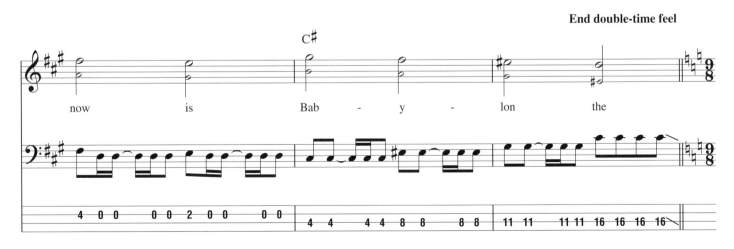

Outro

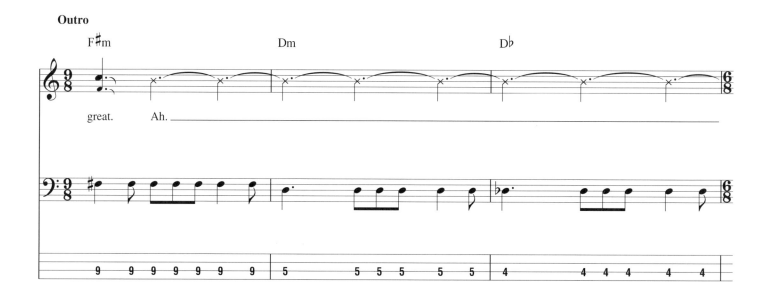

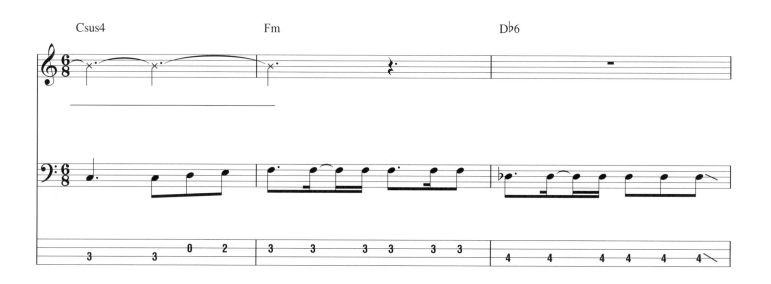

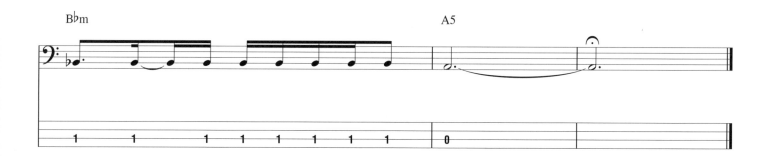

Additional Lyrics

2. The city dressed in jewels and gold,
Fine linen, myrrh and pearls.
Her plagues will come all at once as her mourners watch her burn.
Destroyed in an hour.
Merchants and captains of the world,
Sailors, navigators too
Will weep and mourn this loss with her sins piled to the sky.
The beast and the harlot. Oh.

Scream

Words and Music by Matthew Sanders, James Sullivan, Brian Haner, Jr. and Zachary Baker

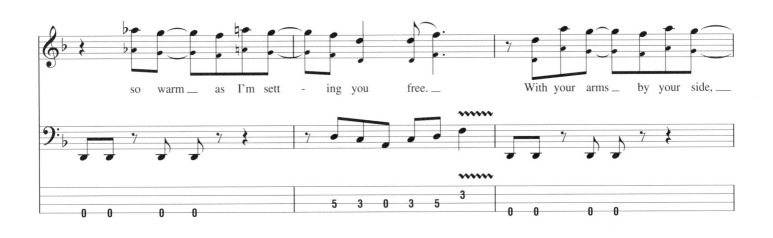

so warm __ as I'm sett - ing you free. __ With your arms __ by your side, __

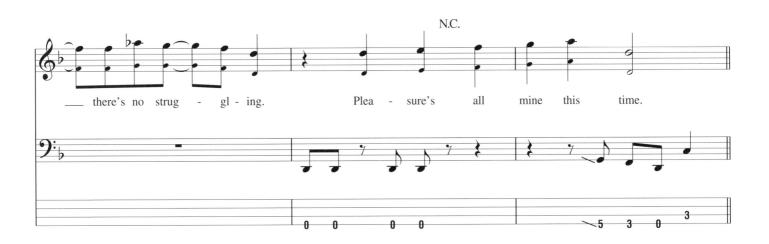

N.C.

__ there's no strug - gl - ing. Plea - sure's all mine this time.

Pre-Chorus

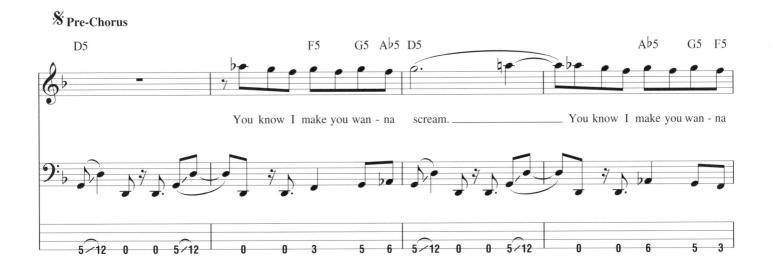

D5   F5   G5   A♭5   D5   A♭5   G5   F5

You know I make you wan - na scream. __ You know I make you wan - na

D5   F5   G5   A♭5   E♭5   D5

run from me, ba - by, but now it's too late. You've wast - ed all your time. __

Verse

3. We've all __ had a time __ where we've lost __ con- trol. We've all __ had our time __ to grow. __

D.S. al Coda 1

N.C.

I'm ho - pin' I'm wrong, __ but I know __ I'm right. I'll hunt a - gain one night.

Coda 1

Guitar Solo
Half-time feel

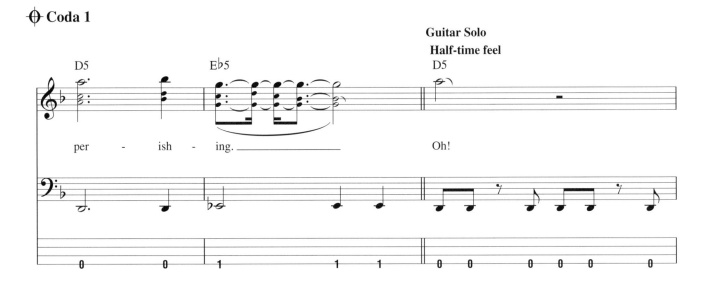

per - ish - ing. _____ Oh!

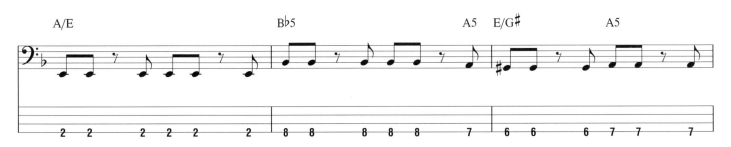

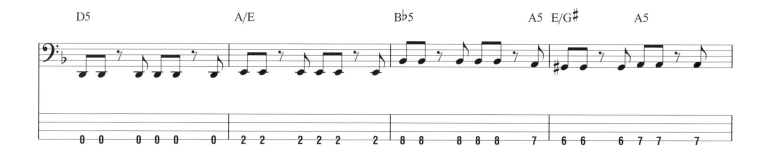

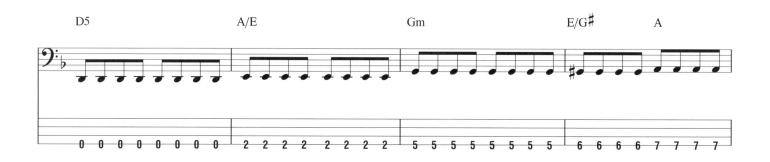

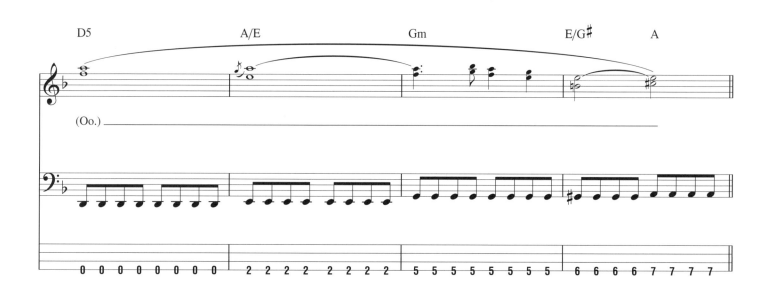

Bridge

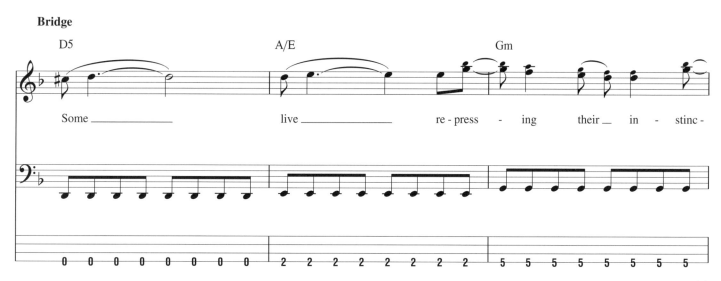

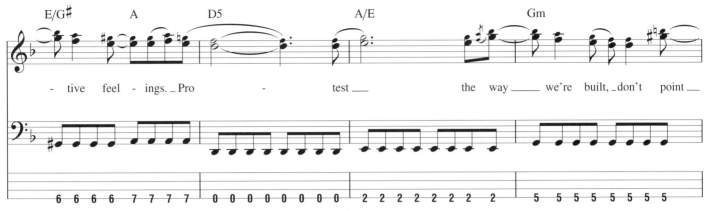

End half-time feel

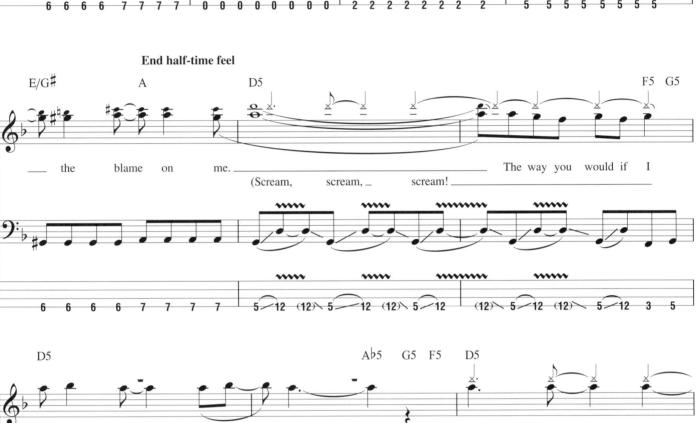

D.S.S. al Coda 2

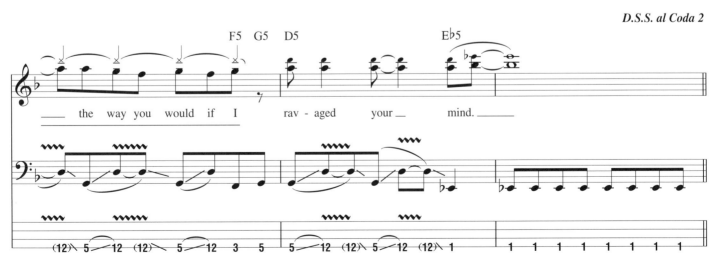

Unholy Confessions

Words and Music by Matthew Sanders, James Sullivan, Brian Haner, Jr. and Zachary Baker

Drop D tuning:
(low to high) D-A-D-G

Intro
Fast ♩ = 180

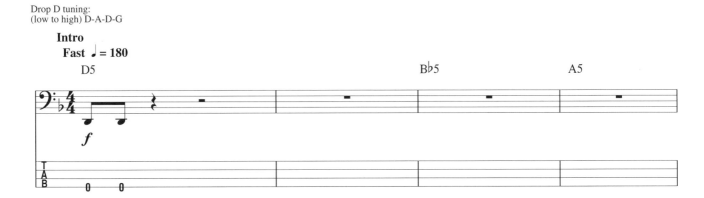

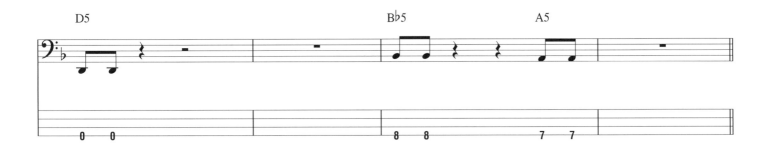

Double-time feel

1., 2., 3.

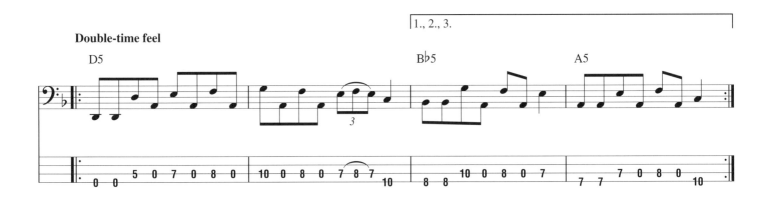

4.

Verse
End double-time feel Half-time feel

Screamed: "I'll try."

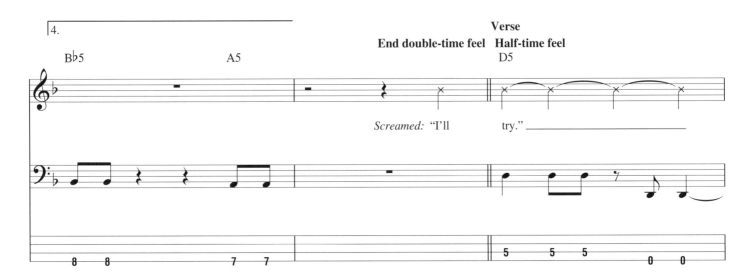

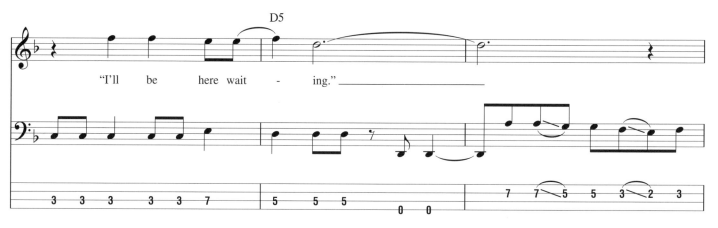

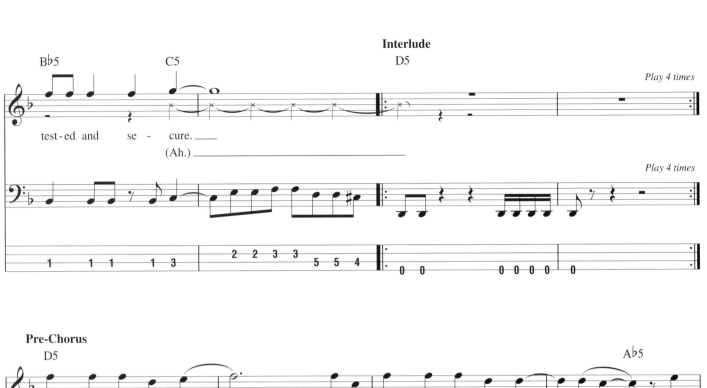

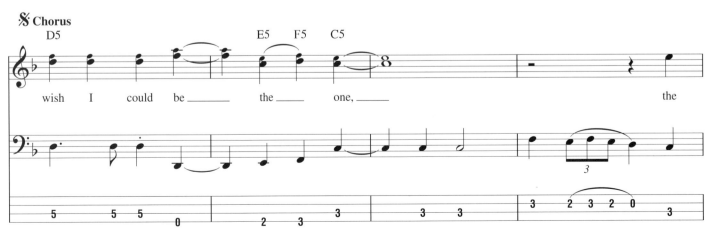

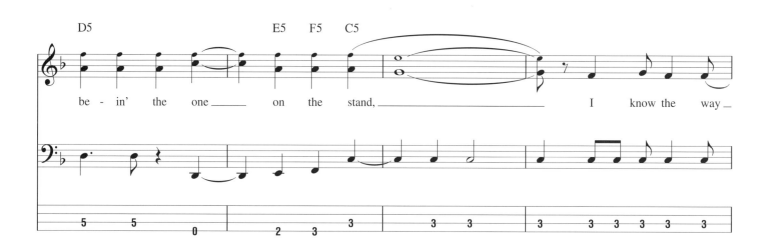

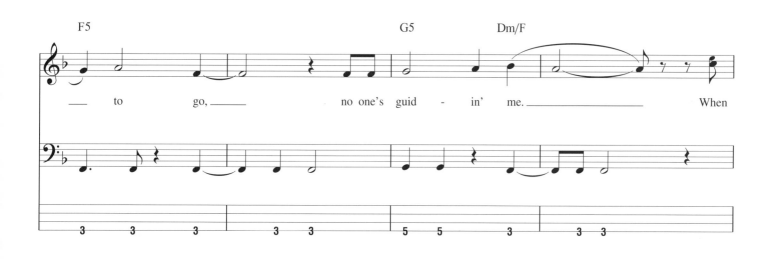

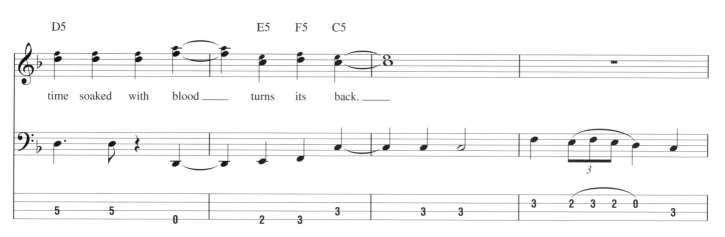

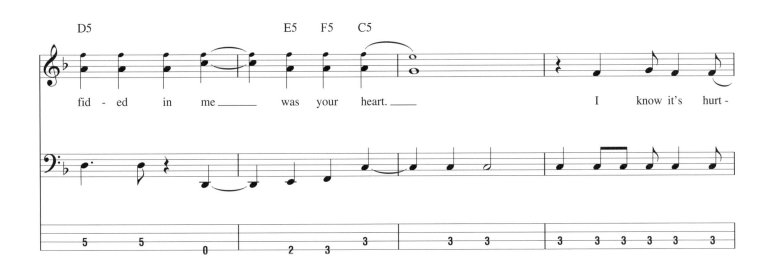

To Coda ⊕

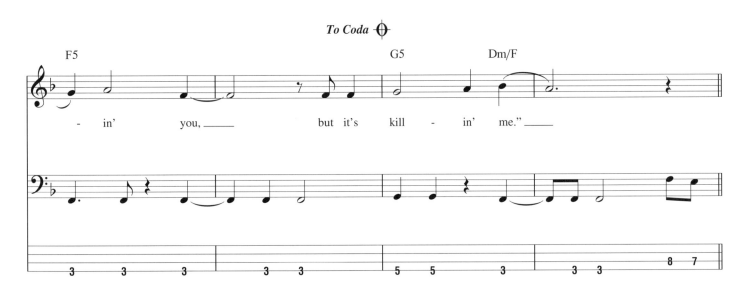

Interlude

End half-time feel

Bridge
Double-time feel

Screamed: Noth - ing will last in this __ life, our time is spent con-struct - ing.

Now you're per - fect - ing a __ world meant to sin. _____

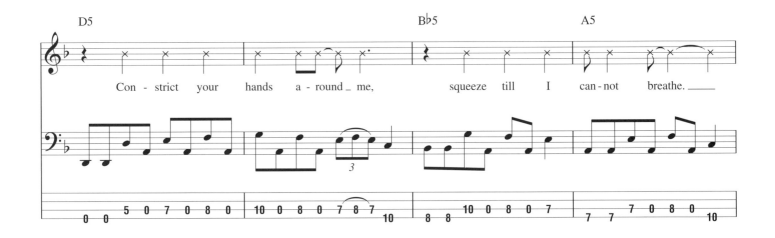

Con - strict your hands a - round me, squeeze till I can - not breathe.

End double-time feel

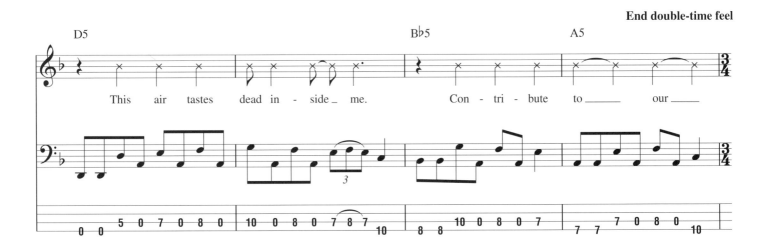

This air tastes dead in - side me. Con - tri - bute to our

Half-time feel

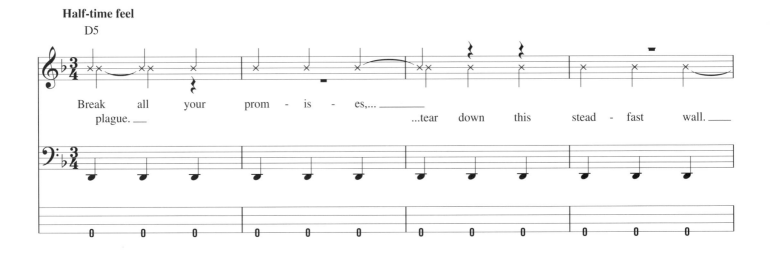

Break all your prom - is - es,... ...tear down this stead - fast wall.
plague.

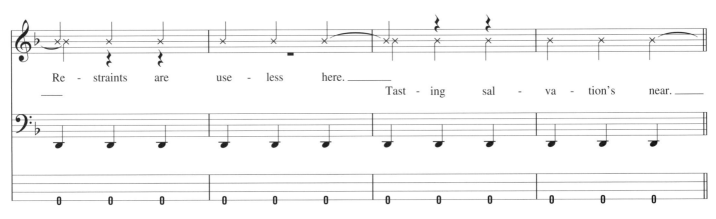

Re - straints are use - less here. Tast - ing sal - va - tion's near.

Interlude

D.S. al Coda

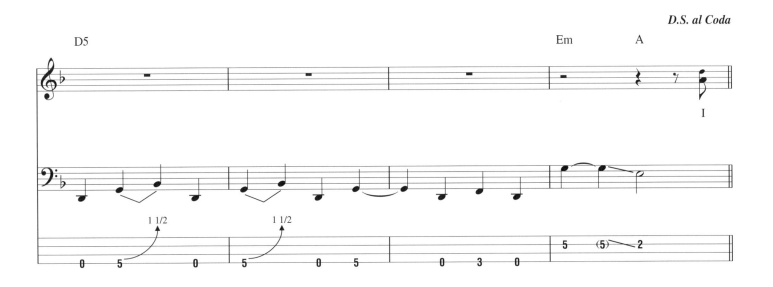

Coda

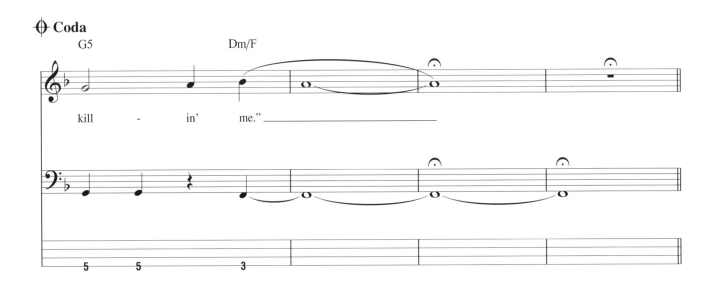

kill - in' me." _____

Outro

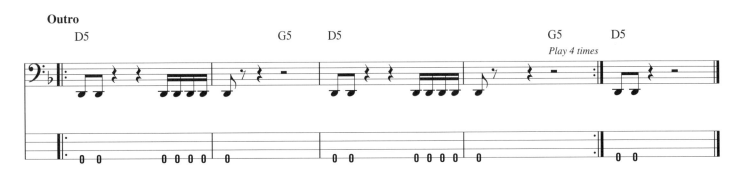